7-75

THE NECESSARY MAJORITY:
MIDDLE AMERICA AND THE
URBAN CRISIS

The Necessary Majority: Middle America and the Urban Crisis

ROBERT C. WOOD

Columbia University Press

NEW YORK AND LONDON

1972

ROBERT C. WOOD

IS PRESIDENT OF THE

UNIVERSITY OF MASSACHUSETTS.

COPYRIGHT © 1972 COLUMBIA UNIVERSITY PRESS
ISBN: 0-231-03617-5
LIBRARY OF CONGRESS CATALOG CARD NUMBER: 70-183228
PRINTED IN THE UNITED STATES OF AMERICA

In 1956 the Radner Family Foundation established a lectureship at Columbia University in memory of William Radner, a graduate of Columbia College and the Columbia Law School. Since his career in the public service had been terminated by his untimely death, the gift appropriately stipulated that these lectures were to deal with subjects in the field of public law and government. Previous Radner Lectures were:

1959 Harry S. Truman, Former President of the United States
      "The Presidency"

1960 Lord Boothby, Rector of the University of St. Andrew's
      "Parliament and the Profession of Politics in Britain"

1963 Robert R. Bowie, Director of the Center for International Affairs, and Dillon Professor of International Relations, Harvard University
      "Present and Future in Foreign Policy"

1965 Lord Harlech, Former British Ambassador to the United States
      "Must the West Decline?"

1966 Richard E. Neustadt, Professor of Government and Associate Dean in the John F. Kennedy School of Government, Harvard University
      "Alliance Politics"

To Peggy, Franny, Maggie, and Frank,
WITH SPECIAL THANKS FOR THE YEARS
IN CLEVELAND PARK

Preface

PRESIDENT LYNDON JOHNSON and Secretary Robert Weaver were responsible for most of the actions this book describes. To the President I am grateful for constant patience and personal support of some of the highly risky ventures in the launching of the United States Department of Housing and Urban Development. Bob Weaver was a wise friend and considerate colleague, and I count our three years together as a very special time. Cabinet and sub-Cabinet associates contributed to that experience, and above all so did the first five assistant secretaries of HUD: Philip Brownstein, Charles Haar, Donald Hummel, Dwight Ink, and Ralph Taylor. Whatever the ultimate judgments of HUD in its formative period, as the urban crisis of the sixties broke upon us, the department remained a going organization. These men kept it going.

But those who take action do so from a limited perspective. For more detached and precise appraisals of the process of urban development and ways to guide it, others often helped to shape my thinking, two with whom I differ professionally as the first chapter indicates, but in the context of genuine admiration and personal friendship: Edward C. Banfield and Patrick Moynihan. Two more are academic colleagues who reviewed and improved the early drafts of the book: Duane Lockard of the Politics Department at Princeton University, and Herbert Gans, when he was a senior associate of the M.I.T.-Harvard Joint Center for Urban Studies. Joseph W. Bartlett, of Ely, Bartlett, Brown & Proctor, commented from the special perspective of a former Under Secretary of the Department of Commerce. Andrew Bell III gave the views of a professional from the San Francisco Regional HUD office. P. I. Prentice of Time-Life, Inc., provided the insights and knowledge of a life-time study of the American housing industry.

Once again, Nan Senior Robinson served as editor and conscience, improving language and insisting on fact in such a skillful blend as to make the thesis advanced seem at least plausible.

Finally, Margaret Byers Wood continues to understand the not very reasonable demands of authorship, to respond with sympathy and tolerance and to make affectionate allowance. I thank them all.

Boston, Massachusetts   Robert C. Wood
September 24, 1971

Contents

THE NECESSARY MAJORITY:
MIDDLE AMERICA AND THE
URBAN CRISIS

Introduction

Scientists and economists illustrate rates of change by "doubling time." For example, the number of significant scientific discoveries made between 1900 and 1950 equaled all that had been made in the preceeding 2,-000 years; between 1950 and 1970, this number doubled again. Despite the enormous increase in the base number, the doubling time had dropped from 50 to 20 years. For the last 50 years, the doubling time for this nation's electric power output has been one decade—a 32-fold increase overall. It took 500 years for the speed of setting type to go from one to 14 lines per minute; six years to go from 14 to 1,800 lines; and one year to go from 1,800 to 15,000 lines.[1]

Rates of change of this magnitude—and the examples could be expanded to almost all aspects of modern life—tend to make historical continuity irrelevant, and to focus our attention on the future rather than the past or even the present. Perhaps it is for this reason that this period of decreasing technological and economic doubling time has seen a parallel decrease in our national attention span. We seem to whirl through one set of events, episodes, preoccupations after another at an exponential rate. Even our acknowledged national crises seem disposable—a moment of exhilarating involvement, a media-induced tickle to the national fancy, then flop under the table with yesterday's newspapers.

It is one of these apparently discarded crises—the "crisis of the city"—that these lectures were designed to explore. They were delivered in April, 1970, under the kind auspices—and bracketed by the generous hospitality—of Columbia University. I had just spent three intensive years at the new Department of Housing and Urban Development after an apprenticeship on three Presidential urban task forces, and this represented an initial effort to come to terms with both the changing fortunes of urban concerns and the national domestic policy process.

America's concern with its cities as it began to surface in 1965 and 1966 was grievously belated. But for the urban poor and the urban professionals who had been there all along, it was also hopeful and energizing.

Four and now five years later, this hope becomes increasingly wistful. The innovative legislation that rode the crest of the wave—model cities, metropolitan planning incentives, rent supplements, urban renewal reforms, national housing goals, encouragement to new towns—has been largely beached by lack of funds, initial disappointments, timidity, and misunderstanding.

Yet such is my middle-aged stance that I remain an anxiety-ridden optimist about the prospects of our really tackling urban problems. In spirit and temper unrevolutionary, unshaken by cries of doom, I am convinced there are courses of action that taken now and in substantial measure can give most Americans better communities in which to live, and can help the next generation find qualities of urban diversity, vitality, and creative accommodation that are better than before.

By acknowledging the seriousness of our problem, I would separate myself from those who counsel self-satisfaction. By undertaking to "solve" the problem, I hope to escape the company of contemporary polemicists.

My natural bias is that of a political scientist. What follows here is a conditional reliance on analysis, on fact, on logic, in contrast to emotion and intuition. Yet theoretical formulations in the social sciences—particularly those couched in the format of lectures and essays—are uncertain vehicles. I do not offer here statistical tables, mathematical models, material for computer simulation. I offer certain events as I knew them and some conclusions about what's wrong with our capacity for urban policy-making.

My hope is to revive a debate that died too soon. The stakes are the future of domestic America.

Chapter I

The Rise and Fall of the Urban Crisis

Writing his love song to New York in 1949, E. B. White caught the promise of the city: [2]

New York blends the gift of privacy with the excitement of participation; [it] is peculiarly constructed to absorb almost anything that comes along without inflicting the event on its inhabitants; so that . . . the inhabitant is in the happy position of being able to choose his spectacle and so conserve his soul.

By the 1960's, the promise seemed to have vanished and the songs to Gotham were seldom affectionate. "New York," observed Fred Powledge, "has become irredeemably, irretrievably rotten.[3]

The nation is finding out how difficult it is to live in the cities and the inmates of New York, being in the most difficult of all cities are finding out quicker and more. . . . There is nothing, literally nothing, that an individual citizen can do that would make New York more livable for

more than an instant. Not even if he is the Mayor. You
soon learn to question your own motive for staying: Are
you *really* demonstrating your belief in cities, your faith
that large groups of people can live in peace, or are you
some kind of masochist?

Or, as the Manhattan druggist put it during the
mail strike:

So the mail don't come. The trains don't come either, and
the phones don't ring when you want them to. That's New
York, pastrami and dirt.

These drastic changes in the condition and out-
look of the urban middle class were paralleled by an
increasing desperation and anger on the part of the
urban poor. And the result was that for three years between 1966 and 1969, the nation acknowledged, belat-
edly and briefly, the existence of an "urban crisis" and
the long, cold slide of New York—in company with
America's other large metropolitan areas—toward
collective vulnerability and despair.

In August 1967, meeting in Washington hard on
the heels of the Newark and Detroit disorders, one
thousand hastily assembled businessmen and state and
local officials declared that the problems of our cities
deserved first priority in the attention of national leaders and in the allocation of budgetary resources. Dis-
satisfied with the pace and depth of national urban assistance programs, they established "The Urban
Coalition," formally uniting influential persons from
both private and public sectors and from both parties

in an effort to build and rebuild better American communities.

A guardedly hopeful National Commission on Urban Problems, headed by former Senator Paul H. Douglas, reported in 1968: [4]

Perhaps the characteristic phenomenon of American politics in the 1960's will some day be seen as the emergence of the city as a political issue.

At first, event tumbled after event to confirm Douglas' judgment:

—Capitalizing on prototype programs in rent supplements and model cities, the national administration doubled the production of public housing units and began drafting the 1968 Housing and Urban Development Act that within a year would increase the annual rate of housing production for the poor by a factor of six compared to the decade of the 1950's.

—The life insurance companies pledged, committed, and spent one billion dollars to underwrite subsidized housing and jobs, and then committed another one billion.

—Old controversial programs were turned around through neighborhood development programs in urban renewal and through tenant participation and home ownership in public housing.

—Congress passed the 1968 Civil Rights Act, including the "fair housing" provision.

—Powerful interest groups in management and labor changed their budgets and internal organizations to give effect to new urban commitments.

—The weekly and daily press as well as radio and television announced special arrangements to cover urban affairs systematically—and sometimes even provided the staff to support such coverage.

Other events intensified the sense of crisis:

—The murder of Martin Luther King;
—The Washington riots and the Cleveland shoot-out;
—The murder of Robert Kennedy;
—Resurrection City.

By 1969, the efforts to respond to root causes— racism, political powerlessness, bad housing, bad schools, bad transportation—were fairly under way, though conditions were still much the same when Douglas described the urban problem as "the big-city slum, and as the white suburban noose, but also as all the problems of growth and population shifts and sprawl and public expenses connected with them." The indices of discontent and protest—on campaign trail, on campus, and in ghetto—still seemed reliable; the conditions, the causes, the mood among those suffering social deprivation remained much the same.

Yet today, after only three years, 239 riots later, 642 politically inspired demonstrations later, 30 million purchases of firearms later, the urban crisis seems to have disappeared. Funds for housing and education have been sharply cut back. Media attention wanders: The ghettos, though not rebuilt nor even maintained, seem quieter. The attention of the nation is elsewhere, focused on the "great question of the seventies," as President Nixon stated it in his State of the Union Address: "Shall we make our peace with nature . . . restoring nature to its natural state?"

In brief, just as we enact the legislation, painfully and haltingly mobilize the resources, slowly gear up organizations, move from strategy to tactics—settle down to work—the alarm sounds for another crisis. Off we charge into a possibly encompassing, certainly distracting, clearly more appealing quest for a better environment.

Now, a better environment is devoutly to be desired. All of us today should be concerned about the dangers from automobile exhaust, the threats from pollution by industrial plants and power stations, the damage inflicted by careless use of chemicals, the need to preserve natural beauty.

But all the advocates of the new environmental priorities should remember that environment, by definition, surrounds the places where Americans live—the great American cities included. Eighty per cent of us live and work chiefly in the urban environment, and our surroundings are more manmade than natural. It is a curious twist. For twenty years the nation failed to provide the most elementary feature of a liveable environment—the decent housing guaranteed by the

1949 Housing Act. Now conveniently setting aside this failure, it passes on to a concern over other aspects of the environment. It is as if this country is doomed to aspire to one impossible dream after another, without ever taking seriously the effort to make these dreams attainable. Increasingly, the American mood seems now one of a temptation to talk, to pass legislation, to beat the drums for new policies—but never, never to put the policies and legislation into action. Increasingly, environmental escapism appears one way in which we submerge our present responsibilities and obligations.

How did we come to this kind of politics of escapism? Is it possible to change our politics to emphasize the actual resolution of problems rather than their rhetorical identification? How can we come to grips specifically with urban problems? These are the issues to which this volume addresses itself.

In brief, I would argue that the politics of escapism comes about not because, as some suggest, the urban issue is a phony one, nor because, as others say, our political system is too rigid and self-satisfied to deal with urgent problems. Instead, I suggest that a complicated system undertaking to resolve a complicated problem does not immediately calibrate—and has difficulty in matching—the challenge and the response. Especially does a majoritarian system come uneasily to the resolution of a minority problem.

In the case of urban affairs, economic and political

needs of minorities and majorities have become confused. And economic and political responses have been mismatched. We have not sorted out when and how to apply appropriately the two great techniques of governments—*law* and *subsidy* (or regulation and resource allocation).

Elemental minority needs—psychological and economic—that first provoked the urban crisis have stimulated majority fears. Majority needs now seem likely to intensify minority fears. Before effective progress can be made, we will need to understand majority and minority urban requirements, and we will have to understand whether old-style or new-style politics—politics that we will term "distributive" and "innovative"—can best satisfy them.

Put baldly, the principal propositions I wish to make are:

—The urban crisis has not in fact disappeared.
—It deserves major attention.
—It can be substantially resolved.

To be persuasive, however, we will need first to explain why the crisis seems to have disappeared.

Chapter II

The Nonexistent Problem:
You're All Right, Jack

Influential and powerful voices today argue that there is not now—and never has been—an urban crisis. Present and former colleagues, in Cambridge and Washington, fall broadly into the category of historical relativists and mournful aristocrats who see our urban world as the best that is possible. Optimistic economists occasionally occupy the same terrain, principally because by treating matters on the broader national and international scale local difficulties are averaged out.

Edward Banfield and Daniel Moynihan are our most visible and engaging spokesmen for the nonexistent crisis. Together, counseling benign neglect of our unheavenly cities, they are representative and eloquent advocates of the thesis of the unreal urban problem.

Moynihan's first "lost" memorandum bristled with righteous facts and figures as to the progress of the black and the poor during the 1960's. And Banfield's latest book, *The Unheavenly City,* documents selectively both the relative improvement in substandard housing between 1950 and 1960 and the heartening attitude among Negroes sampled in 1964 that things were getting "better."

Moreover, both authors remind us that, whatever our problems, our urban ancestors were far worse off. Banfield, in particular, graphically describes the sordid, unplanned, chaotic conditions of nineteenth-century New York and Boston and laconically traces the futility and frustration of efforts to reform them at that time.

No matter that the record production year of the American housing industry was 1950—twenty years ago!—when we once achieved an annual rate of two million units. Set aside the recent Rand Institute report which indicates that rental housing in New York is in a state of near-paralysis. No matter that over the last twenty years federal subsidies for urban transit were at the ratio of 1 to 200 in comparison to highways, and an adjustment in policy might conceivably have altered both the pattern of urban development and the comfort of urban travelers. Whatever the present state of urban housing, urban transportation, urban health, urban crime, *somewhere* in the past, *something* was worse.

As Banfield sees it, the urban crisis is only the unfortunate result of unrealistically elevated expectations and redefinitions of adequacy.[5]

At the turn of the century when almost everyone was a "dropout," the term and the "problem" did not exist. It was not until the 1960's when for the first time a majority of boys and girls were graduating from high school . . . that the "dropout problem" became acute. . . . Obviously, if one defines the "inadequate amount of schooling line" as that which places one-fifth of all boys and girls below it, then one-fifth of all boys and girls will always be receiving an inadequate amount of schooling. . . . To a large extent . . . our urban problems are like the mechanical rabbit at the race track, which is set to keep just ahead of the dogs no matter how fast they may run. Our performance is better and better, but because we set our standards and expectations to keep ahead of performance, the problems are never any nearer to solution.

More than an historical time sense lies behind the Banfield-Moynihan position of a spurious crisis. The position is, in fact, based on a deep-rooted, profoundly pessimistic model of man, class-oriented but along non-economic principles of classification. Moynihan's "underclass," Banfield's "lower-class"—the lumpenproletariat—are for them the real source of our urban difficulties. Their unsalutary impact is compounded by misguided liberal public policies designed to help them.

The case that the lower class is the root of all evil has never been more engagingly advanced. From Edwardian phrase-making to Victorian smugness, to quotations of defenders of the British rotten-borough system that helped spark the American Revolution, one is led back to treating a sizable portion of the urban population in subhuman terms. Indeed, as one traces Banfield's mournful analysis of the lower class, which he defines as characterized by an inability to discount time and a disinclination to discipline, and reads his wistful hope that perhaps many of them will not procreate because few of them will aspire, one recalls the whole nineteenth-century genre of hypocritical lament on the immorality of the poor.

It is with a sense of some continuity that one arrives at the quotation from Simon Newcomb (1886) that introduces the chapter on "The Future of the Lower Class." [6]

If the children of the degraded classes could be taken in infancy before their bad habits have had time to form, and trained to earn a livelihood, a certain proportion of them would be redeemed. If those who could not be so trained were allowed to starve, the number to grow up a burden on society would be diminished. . . .

Banfield's own characterization of the urban "lower class"—as distinct from the "working," "middle," and "upper" classes—sounds almost as if it might have come from one of Mr. Newcomb's contemporaries: [7]

The lower-class individual lives from moment to moment. If he has any awareness of a future, it is of something fixed, fated, beyond his control: things happen *to* him, he does not *make* them happen. Impulse governs his behavior, either because he cannot discipline himself to sacrifice a present for a future satisfaction or because he has no sense of the future. He is therefore radically improvident; whatever he cannot consume immediately he considers valueless. His bodily needs (especially for sex) and his taste for "action" take precedence over everything else—and certainly over any work routine. He works only as he must to stay alive. . . .

Because being "present-oriented" is not the *result* but the *cause* of poverty and disorder and is essentially irremediable, public policies designed to help the poor usually make things worse. As bad money drives out good, poor children cheapen good schools, poor workers reduce productivity, leniency and understanding beget crime, better housing is misused, public libraries and museums are unappreciated. Banfield's most arresting prescription is for semi-institutional care for the semicompetent, although he concedes that this and most of his other recommendations (e.g., "Abridge to an appropriate degree the freedom of those who in the opinion of a court are extremely likely to commit violent crime") are politically "unacceptable."

There are important variations in analysis between Banfield and Moynihan. Moynihan is less comforted than Banfield by historical urban progress, and his American underclass is Negro—its present dilemma, the deterioration of family life, is rooted in slave history. Banfield's lower class embraces both black and white. Both, however, are pessimistic as to the prospects for improvement.

If there is an urban crisis, by these accounts, it is only because a larger number of the poor have been attracted to large cities recently, and their concentration geometrically encourages their misbehavior. But, given the intractability of the underclass, nothing much can be suggested—this condition is a difficulty to be endured, not a problem to be solved.

Beyond the poor, Banfield sees mostly inconveniences in development processes for the rest of urban America—in housing, journey to work, the use of land, the provision of public services, the assurance of clean air and water. In these areas, the market mechanism does the best it can and is in any case superior to any kind of public intervention. Moynihan would frame a national urban growth policy, but it would concentrate on avoiding cities, at least existing ones, as much as possible.

Problems of Logic and Evidence

Now, just as these lectures, the Banfield and Moynihan contentions are essentially essayist. Yet, even these tentative formulations raise problems in logic and evidence. Banfield's concept of class is unorthodox—abandoning objective measures of condition and attitude for a concept of time that most sociologists treat as a function of economic opportunity. Moynihan's emphasis on the Negro family has a ring of historical reasonableness but its statistical reliability is open to considerable question.

Indeed, one can contrast these assertions of the inevitability of the lower class with John Gardner's well-documented commitment to individual and social excellence. Where Banfield sees aimless, sensate behavior, Gardner finds the forces of egalitarianism and competitive performance overriding hereditary limitations. Carefully distinguishing between intelligence in the academic sense and "the many kinds of excellence," insisting on the American fact of a wide dispersal of leadership, his depiction of our urban society has qualities of change and optimism.[8]

To be generous, the hard evidence about the underclass, so far as social science can be said to be hard, yields mixed inferences. James Coleman's report on education, produced under pressure, together with Arthur Jensen's research findings on I.Q.'s and their rebuttals,[9] goes a long way to refute the old simplistic correlations between educational investment and achievement that the presently besieged liberal intelligentsia is accused of having accepted. But they do not suggest, by any kind of reliable time series, the permanence of the differentials established; nor do they confirm the Banfield hypothesis that the old tenement trail only worked for the "Wasp" who was luckily there first or the Jew who was chosen and therefore complete with mother and discipline. In contrast, what Oscar Handlin, Sam Warner, and other urban historians have established is that, although the melting pot has not produced a homogenized America, it has

moved generations of one ethnic group after another
into the ranks of middle America.

Indeed, the facts of Negro economic progress set
forth by Moynihan, as well as the last seven Council of
Economic Advisers' reports, cast considerable doubt on
the idea of an underclass growing larger. The careful
motivation studies of McClelland and his associates [10]
show no confirmation of its passivity (although they record the inappropriateness of much school philosophy
these days). Put mildly, they give one pause in at-
tempting to lump together the evidence of race, economic class, and personality structure to yield a single
category of causation in a world we know to be complex, dynamic, interconnected, and subtle.

At rock bottom, two facts about modern urban
America stand out: First, its black newcomers have a
history as victims of the nation's collective indecency
so special as to suggest that their situation is unique.
Second, the American social structure, outside the an-
tebellum south, has never included class in the British
sense, employed as a means of governance. It is a very
different matter to stratify a society by those who entered some time ago and never rose, or were discarded,
than to stratify according to dates of arrival and pre-
dict that the latest newcomer is the surest to fail as
time goes by. Migration—farm to city, laborer to
manager—is a persistent, powerful, ceaseless fact of
American life, the predominant force in our urban experience.

Whatever their analytical and empirical shortcomings, however, the urban disbelievers make a valuable, powerful contribution: They focus our attention on the concentration of the poor in inner cities as an indisputable special characteristic of our present urban crisis. But they do so at the price of misreading the evidence of class mobility and excluding other factors that seem important—economics, racism, migration, tradition, land facilities, and style. They leave us accounting for our discontent by suggesting that we expect too much out of life. More precisely, they accuse us of being American liberals "born free" in the sense of Louis Hartz, not European conservatives, in the tradition of Herbert Spencer. Fundamentally, they contend that it is the urban observer, not the urban condition, that is out of whack.

Chapter III

The Unworkable System: Evil or Out-of-Date

If one *is* an American, perhaps even of populist persuasion, expecting the next generation to do a little better than the last, admitting the possibility of tragedy but not relishing it, and persisting in believing in an urban crisis, the next question is tougher. If the crisis is real, why did it recede from public attention: one national election, one new crisis of the environment, and gone like the Wizard of Oz?

A second explanation then, in contrast to the absence of the problem, turns on the unworkability of our system in doing anything about the American city. Ruffles and flourishes, rhetoric, and talk, are, in the view of some, all that politicians are capable of. After the poor and the black believed for a while, disillusionment and cynicism set in. Before the Kerner Commission Kenneth B. Clark remarked on the similarity of the reports on the 1919 Chicago riots, the 1935 and 1943 Harlem riots, and the 1965 Watts riot: [11]

I must again in candor say to you members of this commission—it is a kind of Alice in Wonderland with the same moving picture reshown over and over again, the same analysis, the same recommendations and the same inaction.

Variations on this theme are not wanting. From the polemical indictments of the New Left to the detailed dissections of governmental frailties in metropolitan areas published by the Committee for Economic Development, the American political system is under savage attack today.

Witness after witness in the Douglas Commission hearings sought to lay the blame for urban conditions on federal red tape and delay. Analysis after analysis in the Kerner and Kaiser reports documented the inability of state and local government to respond to the ghetto. Where reformers during the thirties looked to government as an instrument for compassionate help, today that faith is little evident. Cabinet secretariats, governors' staffs, mayors' offices join Wall Street, *Time-Life*, David Rockefeller, and the Mafia as members of the "establishment"—the enemy.

One of the most discerning general critics of the system, Herbert Gans, has questioned whether a majoritarian system, dependent on the general electorate for direction and working through the three tiers of federalism, can ever provide answers to the three elements he sees as comprising the urban crisis: poverty, segregation, and municipal decay. Heavily weighing the effect of white backlash, discounting the electorate's disposition to preserve the central city in its long-term interest, and suspicious of municipal bureaucracy, Gans advocates the extension of the suffrage but, more important, the acceleration of the decentralization process put in motion by the poverty program in 1964. One of his solutions for the apparent unmanageability of the inner city is to break the core up into manageable proportions and equip each bailiwick with command over vital services and facilities. Another tier of federalism, a redrafting of boundary lines to fit the territorial imperative of the latest newcomer, might, in his judgment, allow the new minorities their just due.[12]

That this divide-and-live-in-peace doctrine has innate appeal is clear: The political identity of American suburbs rests on the grass-roots symbolism. Applied as Gans suggests, however, it continues and intensifies some long-standing suburban difficulties.

First, territorial conversion of minorities to majorities can bring political power without program power. That is, the neighborhood jurisdiction is often too small to permit effective direction of urban development or redevelopment. Land values, housing markets, jobs, the availability of public resources are not—and *cannot*—be solely determined within neighborhoods. The neighborhood industry, the neighborhood school, the neighborhood health center are cottage industries, little red schoolhouses, first-aid stations—they can rarely absorb the technology that solves problems. So "community control" can mean community nonperformance —with disastrous psychological and economic results.

Second, territorial conversion in the late twentieth century faces the selfsame political issues Madison identified for the late eighteenth century in *Federalist #10*. Unless urban neighborhoods are joined together in some greater polity that requires interaction, communication, debate, and decision, they are themselves self-contained majorities, contemptuous of any lingering minority. The same defects that prompt Gans' reforms are reproduced in miniature.

So, although deficiencies in the governmental process are clearly numerous, and the majority-minority problem (no longer resolvable in terms of majority "will" and minority "rights") remains to plague us, no easy remedy seems at hand. The system did register throughout the sixties increasing attention to the minorities; it did begin the process of diverting resources; it did undertake a series of responses. If no new directions are persuasively specified by those who totally reject the system, we are still left with our question: What happened to the urban crisis? Faced with genuine, not counterfeit problems—interjected as a major agenda item into the system, not ousted by it—how did our attention wander?

Chapter IV

Minority Needs and Majority Fears

There is at least one other explanation for the case of the disappearing crisis: That is, the system mishandled the problem, missed strategic opportunities, and made some understandable but costly errors. At times of great pressure, when American urban areas and urban institutions were undergoing profound changes, some aspects of urban discontent were misinterpreted and others ignored. Accordingly, some public prescriptions were misapplied, and some ills went untreated. More fundamentally, start-up costs were often mistaken for average costs over time, and initial misdirection seemed testimony to permanent program failures.

At best, the American political system, divided as it is in its power (in order to assure liberty and restrain precipitous actions), carries out positive programs with some difficulty. The system requires at least passive program acceptance by a majority and indifference or inattention from minority veto groups. In the past, it has handled resource reallocation and subsidy duties better than direct services or regulation. Above all, it has functioned through most of its history by what can be called "distributive politics." That is, the system has been preoccupied with adjusting and readjusting the relative benefits offered farmers, union workers, large and small businesses, and the professions.

But urban politics in the sixties had few of these features. The clear economic and political needs were those of an obvious, discernible minority, the newest migrants to the central city ghetto. The economic requirements of the white urban majority were being reasonably well satisfied by home insurance and social security programs inherited from the New Deal and the express highway program begun in the 1950's.

More important, the issue was not distribution of a fixed or slowly rising quantity of resources. With a soaring G. N. P., destined almost to double by the end of the decade, the political issue was not only who got what, when, and how but also how additional resources and additional public authority could be used to try to solve problems heretofore neither identified nor believed capable of solution. The Peace Corps was, of course, a glamorous example of the new "politics of innovation"—but the war on poverty, rent supplements, and model cities were of the same character. Predicated on the expectations in 1964 and 1965 that even after Vietnam costs were calculated, a budget sur-

plus of some $12 billion would be forthcoming, the
government's task shifted from justifying the taking of
resources from one group to give another to the question of how to apply an apparently growing dividend
to special purposes and new tasks.

So the system undertook to respond simultaneously to the obviously real economic needs of blacks
pushed off the farms and pulled into the cities and to
the more subtle but urgent political and psychic demands for identity, place, and purpose in the society.
To satisfy the former, it had principally the welfare
and unemployment systems designed for majoritarian
needs of the Great Depression. To satisfy the latter, it
had principally the idealist concepts of citizen participation blended in the latter days of the New Frontier
from an unquestioned belief in grass-roots ideology
and an unrestrained scorn of bureaucracy and professional service workers.

Some of that recent history is recapitulated in the
next chapter in order to suggest how a second attack
on the urban problem might begin. Here, it is enough
to identify the two complications that caused our politics the greatest difficulty: (1) the confusion between
economic development and community development
programs, and (2) the failure to develop an urban strategy as obviously responsive to the "innovative" needs
of the majority as of the minority.

The Kerner Commission offers perhaps the best
example of coupling a political diagnosis with an eco-

nomic prescription. Having made "racism" the root cause of urban disorder, and finding America moving toward two nations, separate and unequal, its remedy was more money—billions for housing and welfare. In a similar vein, the poverty program never faced up to the fact that the need for community control had to balance with the professional requirements for program production—the fact that some place, some time, housing needed to be produced, schools opened, plans executed.

In short, in a system where many players scarcely recognized the new nature of their politics or the character of their constituencies, leadership plunged in, behaving as if the rules of the old game still applied. Little wonder that, at least initially, disillusionment and cynicism accompanied both community and economic development.

When unfilled minority needs, intensified by rising expectations and compounded by a low level of capability in urban institutions, sputtered in disorders in 1965 and 1966 and exploded in August, 1967, majority fears crystallized, were articulated, and found political expression. The relative absence of workable innovative programs outside the ghetto, the unwillingness of the white suburbanite to calculate his existing subsidies, his frustration at the lack of appreciation by the poor, changed majoritarian attitudes from indifference to indignation. Wallace became the critical factor for Nixon and Humphrey as minority and majority indignation collided. "So much talk, so little action," said the poor. "So much welfare, so little appreciation," retorted the "hard-hats."

The Johnson Administration's wide knowledge of the Washington subsector of urban politics gleaned from painful experiences in past battles, momentum, and sheer luck pushed the 1968 Housing and Urban Development Act through the Congress in the Indian summer of Johnson's term. But the thrust and drive and zeal that accompanied the Washington meeting of August, 1967, seemed suddenly gone. Majority fears overrode minority needs and on its first domestic tryout, the politics of innovation proved too much for the American system to manage.

Chapter V

Reviving the Crisis

If the urban crisis is real, not illusionary, not dead, only resting ominously, barely beneath the surface of our anxieties and discontents, responsible for much of our ills and divisions, America cannot afford to limp along tolerating its miseries. Our system needs to revive the interest in urban affairs, work seriously to resolve pressing issues of racism, deprivation, and noncommunity behavior. In brief, we have a task of political craftsmanship ahead, precedent to the actual building and rebuilding of cities. We have to learn how to make our genuinely new politics of innovation work.

We have to realize that our resources grow faster than our population; that our collective capacity to fashion and carry out programs is expandable; that new assignments can be undertaken by national, state, and local government without reducing the responsibilities of the other levels.

Beyond Majoritarianism

Two characterizations of American politics are fashionable these days: pluralistic and monolithic. Probably the majority of professionals view the outcomes of political contests and the output of governmental programs as the result of compromises and bargains among interest groups more numerous than two. The usual classification is by economic association or to a lesser extent ethnic background; the typical depiction is one of legislative logrolling or gaining command of a program bureaucracy. So numerous are the interest groups, however, so amenable to negotiation and revision, so visible their efforts that their politics, while sometimes sordid, are nonetheless "open."

In sharp contrast to the pluralistic view is the resurging doctrine of the monolithic establishment. With antecedents stretching back at least to the Muckrakers (and probably all the way back to Jacksonian Democracy), the contention that "they" run America finds new fashion today. Variations on the theme now differ from old models of robber barons and city bosses: witness the characterization of the pervasive white-collar organization by C. Wright Mills or the community power structure by Floyd Hunter. The popular quasi-marxist reformation makes business, government, and organized labor all part of the selfsame system, fighting

over the spoils but leaving out the rest of society. At
the heart of the argument that there is an "establishment" lies the assertion that a common pattern of political socialization, a common cultural indoctrination, a
common infusion of a homogenized point of view en-
compass us all. This is also the justification for radical
action by a counterelite as the only plausible approach
to depriving an existing elite of its monolithic power.

Now, of course, neither formulation expresses
American politics as it is although both help to clarify a
complex process. Interest groups *are* active in obtain-
ing benefits and avoiding penalties; common objectives
and standards *do* tend to produce a consensual environment that has overtones of conformity and compul-
sion. But the process of reductionism goes too far when
it omits an entire cast of political actors and when it
obscures how decisions actually occur. One such set of
actors can be identified as "intervening elites," groups
making *professional* contributions to the public policy.
Some elected politicians belong in this category. (Senator Edmund Muskie's contribution to reforming grants-
in-aid is an example, and so is Senator Charles Percy's
development of home-ownership for the poor.) By advancing ideas, intellectuals, academics, consultants, and
journalists occasionally create programs (revenue-sharing, rent supplements, and workfare). Public adminis-
trators interpret policy in important ways and sometimes make policy irresponsibily. Finally, foundations
and churches defy classification as either self-seekers or

mirrors of the society. These forces have to be accounted for in explaining politics.

The process needs elaboration as well. No one who has ever exercised public authority can tell it like it is without emphasizing:

—The importance of information, the simple availability or unavailability of facts. How many slum tenants are there in America? In what part of our metropolitan area is the housing stock deteriorating most rapidly?

—The condition of visibility that surrounds the early analysis of a problem. The idea of a "Comsat" for housing (a high-level business and government collaboration) died after its premature exposure in the *New York Times.*

—The simple fact of party politics. Tortuous choices among projects of equivalent merit are rapidly resolved by the happy accident that some are located in congressional districts of administration supporters.

—The role of ego (Is my career advanced or damaged?) and human fraility. The effect of sheer weariness, anger, or anxiety on the part of the policymaker should not be overlooked.

These factors work *inside* the constraints set by the attitudes of interest groups, public opinion, and the views of other persons in positions with institutional power. The decision-maker anticipates these outside

forces; he rejects some alternatives by predicting probable reactions; he calculates degrees of opposition and
indifference; he undertakes to reconcile personal and
public interests. And he always bites his fingernails in
the process. The politician proceeds always in the
knowledge that the information he possesses is far less
than it ought to be, the time too short for careful con-
templation, the possibility of deception and calculated
misinformation ever present, and the repercussions on
the public and interest groups never capable of thor-
oughly reliable extrapolation. In this process, ideas,
program options, and political acts are driven toward
the simplistic. Elaborate formulations are not compre-
hended by those who must be ultimately involved. Majority acceptance or indifference and minority approval
or disinterest are necessary conditions, yet the time
and understanding of these groups are limited. The
politician's need for tactics cheats his original strategy.

It is in this context that the modern national game
of politics goes on. One can understand the development of a major public program first in terms of
whether it is distributive or innovative—that is,
whether it shifts relatively fixed resources among established interest groups or applies expanding resources to
new concerns and new groups. Then one calculates
whether the program is directed at the majority or the
minority. In this way four analytical categories can be
defined.

I think it is fair to say that most "old school" public programs have been distributive and majoritarian. Omnibus housing and urban affairs bills that provided urban renewal for downtown and home mortgage guarantees for the suburbs in the 1940's and 1950's reflected a distributive strategy of something for everyone (except the poor). Tax reform and tax reduction are classic cases of distributive politics affecting a negotiated "majority" of interest groups and the establishment.

Innovative politics are based on the premise that paying Paul may not require robbing Peter—at least in circumstances of a vastly growing national income. Paul's needs, in fact, may be less a function of economics than of identity, security, status, or political power. It may be the character of a public activity, the nature of an institution that needs to be changed. Perhaps it is a new activity—funded out of expanded resources—that is required. (So it was in the early days of the Great Society when, in addition to securing John Kennedy's long-sought tax cut, Lyndon Johnson moved into entirely new federal activities in education, health, poverty, and urban affairs.) In such cases the politics of innovation can function alongside of distributive politics without fundamental rearrangements. And, like the old politics, the new politics can be beneficial either to the majority (e.g., fluoridation, cancer research) or a minority (e.g., neighborhood legal services, facilities for retarded children).

Two ways exist, then, to respond to an urgent national need. One can identify the interests of a majority of special groups or command the attention of the majority of voters, persuade them of their common concern, and *change the priorities on the national agenda.* This is a popular cry today but an extraordinarily difficult political task, dependent typically on a need emergent in nature and affecting clearly and directly the majority. Foreign affairs and defense excepted, the United States has managed to change the national agenda only twice between the Great Depression and the Eighty-ninth Congress: the interstate highway program and the space program (together with the educational undertakings associated with it) in the immediate post-Sputnik era. Even in these instances, defense considerations blurred the pristine quality of the new priority.

The second method of advancing a new national cause is to *add* to the national agenda in such a way that prevailing priorities are not seriously disrupted. This is the politics of innovation, depending upon a growing supply of economic resources and expanding political energy that permit new public tasks to be defined in ways that usually do not appear to enlarge the scope of government. Here a premium is placed on the performance of the professionals—the intervening elites —and only latterly on the generalized support of interest groups and the public at large.

This was the way in which the urban crisis first received attention in the 1960's from the initial identifi-

cation by John Kennedy to the 1968 Housing and
Urban Development Act, the major legislative achievement of Lyndon Johnson. Operating within the frame-
work of distributive politics, always vulnerable to the
general course of political developments, and open to
the attack that significant resource reallocations had
not occurred, urban politics was innovative, minority
politics in the 1960's. Some of those innovative features
remain intact, but if urban needs are to be met in the
seventies—and in the context of the environmental
challenge—some broader base of support will be required. Reviving the crisis will require pluralism, not
elitism, for the urban problem cannot be resolved by
surplus funding and the attention of urban professionals alone.

Chapter VI

The Ordeal of Innovation

The achievements and and failures of the Kennedy and Johnson administrations, especially the latter, stand today somewhere between often defensive recollections and the beginnings of genuine history. The first barrage of Kennedy memoirs from Sorenson and Schlesinger to Manchester has subsided. The first accounts of the Johnson years are upon us. And both remind us of the difficulties of pinpointing responsibility for policy development—particularly in foreign policy where much of the evidence is classified.

Yet experience and reflection can put flesh on the bones of theory, supplement assertion, and uncover rows of stubborn facts for later historians to reorder. So far as urban affairs are concerned, present knowledge suggests five patterns in the sixties:

—The narrow origins of urban formulations
—The retreat to professionalism
—The urban windfall from the Great Society
—An abortive effort to capture majority support
—Unrealized expectations.

Three men provided continuity in the national conduct of domestic affairs in the sixties: Orville Freeman, Stewart Udall, and Robert Weaver. Early in the Kennedy years, Freeman was able to secure a four-year extension in the major farm subsidies, and in effect he settled his most troublesome political issue. Restless, still reflecting on the decision at the 1960 Democratic National Convention in Los Angeles that removed him from consideration as vice-president, he devoted an increasing amount of his time to international affairs, to the disposition of farm surpluses, and to first steps in developing a sensible national migration policy. "Rural-urban balance" was Freeman's term for it, and however shakily based in economic theory, it provided the beginning for increasing discussions between the Department of Agriculture and the Department of Housing and Urban Development that were to end in common planning legislation in 1968.

Stewart Udall moved in many areas, precursors of the environmental concerns that were to emerge in the late sixties and early seventies. His commission on the Potomac River, his collaboration with Lady Bird Johnson on "beautification," his expansion of the public lands acquisition program gave the Department of the Interior a visibility and sense of motion that it had not had since Teddy Roosevelt.

Unlike Freeman and Udall, Robert Weaver did not begin with Cabinet status. Housing and urban affairs were the responsibility then of the Housing and

Home Finance Administration, a loose confederation of five semiautonomous agencies dealing respectively with public housing, urban renewal, the federal housing guarantee and insurance programs, community facilities, and the Federal National Mortgage Association. Weaver's legislative base was the 1949 omnibus housing act—a major achievement of the Truman administration that represented a "coalition" of Robert Taft and Robert Wagner and the first explicit recognition of the need for government intervention in housing. But the Eisenhower years had not dealt kindly with the goals of that legislation. Public housing starts had been held down to thirty thousand a year, less than half of those originally scheduled, and urban renewal had begun at a much slower pace and with much less interest on the part of all but a few large cities than the framers of the legislation had originally intended.

Weaver faced the problem of assuming command over agencies accustomed to going their own way and executing a law for which funding had never been adequate. Even his right to the job of HHFA administrator had been challenged. As the first high-level Negro appointee of the Kennedy administration, he had endured two days of grueling, abrasive nomination hearings, led by Southern senators. It was a beginning designed to encourage caution and piecemeal advance.

In these circumstances, the Kennedy administration did not come forward with a comprehensive urban program. A pre-inaugural urban task force, headed by Joseph McMurray, counsel to the Senate Committee on Banking and Currency, served up a round robin of moderate old and new ideas. They ranged from a program of rent certificates that had been first advanced in depression days to support for preservation of urban green belts. While Kennedy gave the task force report a tentative welcome as a means of testing agency responses, Weaver dismissed it as useless. The Kennedy administration moved instead to test the saliency of urban affairs in distributive politics— seeking large increases in renewal and public housing funds in response to the calls of big city mayors.

In addition, the President proposed department status for HHFA and Cabinet rank for Weaver. After some months of hesitation he signed as well the executive order barring discrimination in federally assisted housing. But no major proclamations or change in national priorities on urban affairs emerged from an administration so preoccupied with foreign policy that not a single item of domestic concern was identified in the President's inaugural speech.

The effort to increase the urban share of federal attention via distributive politics was largely unsuccessful. Congress rejected the Cabinet proposal and congressional appropriations committees made sure that the budget increases were insignificant. Increasingly persuaded that frontal assaults on urban problems would not gain political support, disinclined toward head-to-head congressional combat, and uncertain of his status within the Kennedy ranks, Weaver turned increasingly to devising modest new programs in the style of innovative politics.

A thirty-year veteran in Washington bureaucratic politics, adept in maneuver and countermaneuver of a technical nature, and fresh from the sobering experience of administering rent control in New York State, Weaver could work creatively in substantive areas of economics with a strong sense of the politically possible in a manner that few political appointees could equal. The 221(d) (3) Moderate Income Subsidy Program was his major creation at that time; but new development grants for public facilities, for open spaces, and for mass transportation were also launched and carefully shepherded through the appropriate committees.

But none of these measures could be said to constitute a major urban program, and certainly they did not change the allocations of resources and powers among competing claimants. Set against the backdrop of a substantial vacancy rate in housing and optimistic academic predictions about an urban future (James Wilson's article in the *Harvard Alumni Bulletin*, for example, entitled, "There Is No Urban Problem"), they were the foundations of an urban strategy. But they still were bootlegged into the councils of state in the name of housing and public works.

The embryonic antipoverty program, as it devel-

oped in what were to be the last few months of the
Kennedy administration, was a parallel venture in innovative politics. Born in the expectation of a budget
surplus, the idea was clearly to *add* poverty to the
agenda of America's domestic concerns—not to undertake a serious redistribution of power or resources. The
role of Michael Harrington's book, *The Other America,*
in arousing President Kennedy's interest in the problem of poverty has been widely acknowledged. The entire development of the program, in fact, can be read
as a case study in the impact on social policy of the
"intervening elite"—a dozen or so lawyers, economists,
social workers, and "generalists" in the Justice Department, the Council of Economic Advisers, the Budget
Bureau, the Defense Department, and outside of the government. But the antipoverty effort was never really
seen as an "urban" program. JFK had been sensitized
to poverty during the West Virginia primary, and the
bill that finally passed, even the provision for "Community Action," was directed as much at rural as urban
poverty. The focus was on employment (work-training,
business loans, aid to migrant workers) and education
(Head-start, work-study) rather than on community development.

The major attention to urban policy and urban
legislation that began in 1964 was not based on new
popular support or spectacular new diagnoses of city
problems. It was largely the beneficiary of Johnson's
determination to accelerate the pace of domestic re-

form, to complete Kennedy's work, and to carve out his own. Building on a mood of unity and compassion that followed the trauma of the assassination, Johnson led the effort to pass the Civil Rights Act and began a hard-sell campaign on behalf of the "War on Poverty."

While there was a general academic consensus that new urban development programs were in order, the counsel of the urban task force that President Johnson set up in 1964 at the instigation of Bill Moyers and Richard Goodwin remained divided on the question of new federal interventions.

Only the nagging sense that a presidential task force ought to say something to the President and a last-minute coalescence in support of a rent supplement program produced a report. Even that was made unanimous only because fog delayed air travel from the San Francisco airport where a dissenting minority waited impatiently in the lobby.

The following year, a new urban task force materialized, which I chaired as before.[13] In the interim, HUD and rent supplements had been born. The major internal debate of the task force turned on the amount of resources to be made available for urban needs and the degree to which these resources should be concentrated within cities. After discussing proposals ranging from the restoration of Washington, D. C., to a massive Marshall Plan for every city so inclined in the country, the task force recommended concentrating on large slum areas in sixty to seventy cities—the forerunner of the model cities program. Despite divergent views on the human and physical aspects of city building, the group also pressed for more emphasis on resident participation and housing construction in urban renewal.

This compromise pleased neither the purists, who felt that the program should be smaller and experimental, nor the city officials, who wanted help on an across-the-board scale and in large amounts. But it proved to be realistic in terms of congressional reception and prudent in terms of administrative capabilities and dwindling resources for non-Vietnam activities.

Urban policy capability at the Federal level remained limited to a small group: Robert Weaver, Morton Schussheim, Weaver's assistant administrator for program policy, Ashley Ford and Hilbert Fefferman in HHFA and then HUD's General Counsel's Office, and a small staff in the Bureau of the Budget headed by Frederick O'Rourke Hayes.

The fragility of the policymaking consensus reflected popular apathy. An occasional editorial appeared on the urban malaise; an enterprising reporter or two took walking tours with Ed Logue through the slums of New Haven and Boston. But the first magazine issue other than a professional journal devoted entirely to the problems of the city was the *Scientific American* for September, 1965. This was followed, in December, by *Life*'s Christmas issue, which put major emphasis on the city as playground for the upper middle class. No major opinion poll listed urban problems among the nation's top ten concerns; no stirrings of great debate were discernible in Congress.

Rent supplements, residential rehabilitation, model cities, metropolitan councils of governments, aid to new communities—all these were conceived, put forward, and enacted in contradiction to the classic rules of thumb of distributive politics: that a majority receive some benefit, that a coalition of power interests approve, or that some great and sustained sentiment sweep the nation. Conceived in what many observers regarded as excessive secrecy, introduced against the strenuous advice of seasoned politicians, untested and untried at state and local levels, the urban programs were unique in their timing and in their auspices. Rarely before had ideas so little heralded, with so little demand, been launched so rapidly under such adversity. Indeed, so Robert Semple reported at the time, when congressional leaders read the President's message on model cities, the call went back to White House staff, "Have you guys lost your minds?"

The Urban Windfall

What maintained the urban programs was not their innovative character nor the enthusiasm they engendered. What saved the Housing and Urban Development Act of 1965 was the encompassing momentum of other major laws and fundings that *were* distributive in nature and mostly distributive to the majority. The tax cut President Johnson achieved to ratify President Kennedy's new economics, the education laws that permitted support to church as well as state schools, Medicare and Medicaid—all the wondrous acts of the Eighty-ninth Congress carried along the concerns of the cities.

In the ebullient first flush of Presidential power, Johnson conditioned chairmen of senate and house committees alike to "another coonskin on the wall," and, in that mood, the Congress enacted the ideologically unpalatable rent supplements—which offered a way to integrate the poor into standard private housing—and the statistically unfavorable model cities program—which offered initial aid to only 75 of the nation's 2,500 towns and cities.

The 14–13 vote of the Senate Appropriations Committee against rent supplements in 1966, which Weaver turned around, and the 17-vote margin that HUD achieved for model cities in the last weekend of the Eighty-ninth Congress were partially due to intensive lobbying. But the style and thrust were Johnsonian, in a Washington era reminiscent of the New Deal. Urban America was the beneficiary of the political power of a Texan who grasped the promise of the city intellectually but had never directly experienced it. Riding high on the remobilization of distributive politics in the style of the 1930's, President Johnson introduced the innovative politics of the 1960's and supported the urban proposals of 1965 and 1966 until legislation was achieved.

Searching for a Suburban Link

That this legislation emerged as "minoritarian" in impact was due to several factors, but the Johnson administration never saw the problems of the cities solely in minority terms. As early as May, 1964, Eric Goldman, then intellectual-in-residence at the White House, was convening meetings of academics (such as Paul Ylvisacker and myself) and political practitioners (such as Abe Fortas and Horace Busby) to consider the needs of urbanites *and* suburbanites in the interest of a majority-oriented urban program.

The first position paper that Johnson's 1965 Task Force on Urban Problems considered was divided into two parts: (1) "the problem of the 'one-fifth' " (the last phrase stricken and replaced by "the poor"); and (2) "the problem of the 'four-fifths' " (the last phrase stricken and replaced by "those who are not poor"). The members of the task force worked consistently to find ways and means to raise the quality of ordinary life for the majority, as well as to reduce the quantity of deprivation for the minority.

In President Johnson's original "Message on the Cities" on January 26, 1966, this dual theme was maintained. Model cities was advanced as a demonstration project on rebuilding the inner city, and the metropolitan development program as an incentive device that would benefit the suburbs.

The metropolitan development idea never caught on with the media, with the Congress, or with the middle-income majority whose long-range interest it was designed to enhance. The program was eloquently advanced, polished, and defended by Charles Haar, an urban-oriented Harvard law professor who served on the 1965 task force and then as an assistant secretary at HUD. It proposed to give special incentive grants to suburban governments willing to work and plan together on federally assisted physical development activities such as parks, hospitals, highways, sewers, water supply, airports, and community facilities. These grants, of perhaps 20%, would be *in addition to* the federal assistance already forthcoming for this kind of development.

More than any single proposal, this piggy-back incentive grant might have encouraged more rational and coherent development as the suburban exodus went on and on into the seventies. The benefits of such development in lower capital costs, less wasteful land use, and an enhanced living environment are not hard to demonstrate. But practical-minded congressmen found it hard to believe that still another federal grant program was going to save the suburbs *or* save money, and urban liberal leaders as well as the press had their attention riveted on the slums and the ghetto.

When the metropolitan development program was included in the proposed Housing Act of 1966, it became a lightning rod for congressional opposition to the entire bill. At HUD, a strategically distressed high command considered giving up MDP to preserve the rest of the bill. It never came to that, and the bill passed with metropolitan development intact. The appropriations committee, however, still unpersuaded, effectively vetoed the program by appropriating not a single penny for its operation.

Meanwhile, the effort to make a coordinated attack on the inner city ills was in trouble. The Budget Bureau was firmly committed to urban development as a "bricks and mortar" process. During the same appropriations cycle which snuffed out the metropolitan development program, the bureau refused to provide funds for tenant services in public housing, for citizen participation in urban renewal, and for several social service components of the new model cities. The innate difficulties of a coordinated approach were compounded by poor administration in the early days of model cities, by the splitting off of mass transportation to the Department of Transportation, and by the continued separatism of the anti-poverty program. One knowledgeable Washington newsman, when asked in 1966 about the relationship between HUD and the Office of Economic Opportunity, replied: "I'd say it is rather like the relationship between a dog and cat in a barrel." Both new, both jealous of new responsibilities, both deeply committed to their own vision of how to save America, the two urban agencies were—to say the least—somewhat wary of one another. But the failure to bring together the poverty and housing programs within HUD was a loss for both. In particular, it meant that the groups representing the urban poor were to be divided and redivided, and the bridge to majoritarian urban concerns was to remain a narrow and fragile one.

The real enemy of urban rebirth, however, was the waxing of foreign affairs, particularly the war in Indochina, and the consequent waning of domestic considerations. The growing national income, essential to innovative politics, began to be absorbed by the cost of Vietnam.

For the political knowledgeables in Washington, the lobbyists, the interest groups, the journalists, 1966 brought an enlarged concern with urban affairs. In the ten-month fight to pass the housing act, the urban alliance representing some sixty public organizations never before associated with city problems augmented the "old reliables" of mayors, homebuilders, mortgage bankers, and housing reformers. The AFL-CIO did a yeoman job in advocating urban legislation at a time when it was difficult to believe their members made model cities a topic for table talk at supper.

Yet, none of these developments served to crystallize grass-roots, cross-country support for specific programs; none turned the growing anxiety about riots and ghettos, discrimination, hunger, and unemployment into a sustained political force. The long hot summer of 1967 produced eloquent editorials, and isolated cries of despair, but few programatic and legislative ideas. Indeed, the mood of the country was already changing. As the national presidential campaign intensified, signs of backlash and resentment appeared. And one came to recall Mr. Dooley's comment on a much earlier America: "The citizen of Massachusetts does not think much about the American Negro, but if he did, he would not like him."

Recourse to Professionalism

As the agony of the urban minority appeared to be growing and the tolerance of the majority diminishing, deepening national division over Vietnam made it increasingly difficult for the Johnson administration to do anything at all. In this atmosphere, the passage of the Housing and Urban Development Act of 1968 was at least a minor miracle.

Where the 1968 legislation originated and found strength was in the experience, knowledge, and sagacity of the professional urbanists, and, not surprisingly perhaps, the importance of the legislation was to be appreciated almost exclusively by professionals. From the point of view of housing, this was the most important act in fifty years, but few Americans then or now could identify a single provision.

At the center of the development of the 1968 legislation was Robert Weaver. He was aided by a staff of thorough professionals such as Jay Janis, Ashley Ford, and William Ross. They worked closely with the Kaiser committee (formally the President's Committee on Urban Housing), which revived the idea of a "housing partnership" between government and large corporate investors. They worked closely with the Budget Bureau, already worrying about how to keep mortgage credit investments from enlarging the annual federal budget. (As it turned out, by making the Federal National Mortgage Association a private instrument, ten to twelve billion dollars could be "saved" in the budget.) They worked with representatives from the Departments of Labor, Commerce, and the Treasury, and from the Office of Economic Opportunity. They worked with the very knowledgeable staff from the congressional subcommittees concerned with housing, and with a few interested leaders in the banking community. The whole process was, of course, subject to comment by the White House staff and the significant fact was that all of these different parties worked in Washington and knew each other professionally over some period of time.

As HUD ended her shakedown cruise, surer knowledge of personalities and temperaments, clearer appreciation of key power relations, a more highly developed sense of timing, and greater familiarity with process and procedure moved the most complex and expensive housing act in American history from drafting board to law with unexpected speed.

The urban professionals were not, of course, without help. Dr. King's terrible murder in April galvanized new support, not only for the 1968 Civil Rights Act, but for urban legislation as well. The Kerner commission's report calling for six million units of new subsidized housing in five years (increasing existing production by a factor of twelve) made the bill's timetable of ten years seem not only plausible but also prudent. But the nation's major newspapers, soured on the administration, studiously avoided comment or support until the very end; public knowledge and political activity were extremely limited. The Washington community "sensed" that the country would not be ill-disposed to the legislation and did not feel required to test that supposition directly. In the temper of the time, Congress and the professionals preferred to work quietly.

What President Johnson called "The Magna Carta of Housing" passed Senate and House by lopsided majorities, where the 1966 act had only squeaked through. On August 2, 1968, it became the law of the land, even as the administration's power in other areas inexorably ebbed away.

The signing ceremony, witnessed by several thousand HUD employees in front of the dramatic curving facade of their new headquarters building, was a moment of considerable sentiment. After the riots Secretary Weaver had been categorized by the press as too cautious and too conservative. Increasingly, he had found himself in the position of administering programs under attack by the people they were designed to serve, and of trying to undertake new responsibilities under severe budgetary ceilings and with a staff that was largely tradition-oriented. Now, however, he had concluded his public career with the major legislative triumph of the year. In an unusual personal and political victory, Weaver watched the final pen strokes of an act that would reform almost every aspect of the programs he knew so well, and substantially affect the housing industry with which he had worked so long.

Chapter VII

The Return to Majoritarianism

Now in the four-fold classification by which this analysis has been shakily proceeding, the 1968 housing act was an innovative minority measure. That is, it did not drastically reallocate resources or shift priorities and, though its provisions for new communities and some of its grants-in-aid could help entire metropolitan populations, its major thrust was to improve the living environment for the central-city poor. But substantial, expensive programs cannot remain minoritarian in support, in understanding, or even in benefits. If appropriations are to flow, program schedules to be met, and most of all, popular attention and new commitments intensified, the coupling to the majority has still to be made.

It is this ability to win majority support or acquiescence that to so many seems so dubious today. It is the willingness of most Americans to pay in money and controls for qualitatively upgrading their urban circumstances that seems so difficult to achieve. In the context of the silent majority—the troubled "middle," "ethnic," "working" American—it seems enormously difficult to get adequate attention to city problems. It is this perceived political mood of the country that makes the urban crisis seem "out" and the new crusade for environment so appealing. As Jeremy Swift observes: [14]

Talk about improving the environment has obvious political advantages. It is the sort of blanket issue that nobody can take exception to, yet is sufficiently complicated when you get down to it, to baffle the non-expert. The housewife whose washing is covered by a fine black dust or the angler whose stream is gradually becoming an open sewer, provide a vein of indignation for politicians to mine; and the culprits need not be too closely identified.

Concern for conservation brings us together (at least until people realize that their own air conditioners and flip-top cans are in question); deciding the locations of public housing projects, applying fair housing laws, enforcing metropolitan planning standards can pull us apart. This is the present dilemma of the "true" urbanist: One can initiate innovative politics on a minority basis and carry out programs while a majority accepts, supports, or is inattentive to the effort. But what really are the prospects that in the 1970's, in the age of middle America and the new populism, the silent majority will continue the drive for urban revitalization when this means substantial attention to the needs of the nonwhite and the poor?

The Middle American:
(1) First Glance

By any kind of content analysis of the popular press, the response to that question must be pessimistic. The average American today is frustrated with his personal situation, beleaguered by inflation and occupational immobility, fed-up with blacks and students, "hot under the blue collar." As *Newsweek* explained in a 1969 report on "The Troubled American:" [15]

"Despite nine consecutive years of prosperity, many a breadwinner can't forget the specter of the wolf in the carport. . . . With little equity but his mortgaged home and his union card, the white worker is especially resistant to integration efforts that appear to threaten his small stake in the world. . . . Many lower-class whites feel that an unholy alliance has grown up between the liberal Establishment and Negro militants to reshape American life at their expense. . . ."

And on this last point, the magazine quotes Eric Hoffer: "We are told we have to feel guilty. We've been poor all our lives and now we're being preached to by every son of a bitch who comes along. The ethnics are discovering that you can't trust those Mayflower boys."

Writing before Mayor John Lindsay's re-election and during that divisive and rather ugly campaign period, the editors of *Newsweek* thought it quite possible that the country was on the verge of class warfare or a grass-roots right-wing dictatorship.

Although less apocalyptic, Herbert Gans has written with no less conviction of the unlikelihood of urban accommodation: [16]

Most voters . . . are not inclined to give the cities the funds and powers to deal with poverty or segregation. This disinclination is by no means as arbitrary as it may seem, for the plight of the urban poor, the anger of the rebellious and the bankruptcy of the municipal treasury have not yet hurt or even seriously inconvenienced the vast majority of Americans. . . . Since the poor and the black will always be outvoted by the majority, they are thus doomed to be permanently outvoted minorities.

The Middle American: (2) Second Look

Implicit in this harsh picture of middle America and the power and intransigence of the new redneck populism are some critical elements that need to be explicitly examined. Gallup has documented for *Newsweek* that the mood of middle America is one of pessimism (46% believe the country is getting worse), of desire for law and order (85% feel black militants and college demonstrators are treated too leniently), of belief that blacks have too much too soon (65% think blacks have a better chance than people like themselves of getting government financial help when out of work, and 44% think blacks have a better chance for well-paying jobs).[17] Granting this, we still need to ask three questions about the majority's attitude:

—How constant are these views?
—How reliably are they associated with "middle-classness" as determined by income, occupation, and family status?
—Do other more fundamental and positive outlooks lie behind them?

If we sift through the cumulative evidence of middle-class opinion—as measured by almost thirty years worth of assorted polls—several encouraging inferences emerge.

First, alongside of current expressions of depression and racism, we find more hopeful, more tolerant views reflective of the generosity, openhandedness, and optimism documented in the United States since De Tocqueville. Even while complaining about taxes, the middle-class white wants government to move on domestic ills, job training, air and water pollution, medical care, better housing and schools, fighting organized crime and crime in the streets. These expenditures are twice as popular as more highways and defense expenditures, and four times as popular as space exploration.[18]

Even at the height of the backlash reaction to the

Newark and Detroit disorders, the Kerner commission reported that the majority of whites acknowledged and deplored discrimination against blacks in employment and housing. Attitude polls in 1968 showed white city residents overwhelmingly in favor of nondiscrimination in employment (95%) and substantially in favor of free housing choice (62%) and equal school investment (78%).[19]

Second, basic beliefs seem to underly and support this expressed approval of government action to benefit minorities. The Harris Poll of August, 1965, asked respondents to rank the good things in life by their value preferences. For white middle-class citizens, two objectives outweigh by factors of four and two respectively the material advantages of affluent America: "To live in a free country," and "To get children well educated."

At the heart of traditional American values lies the chance to get ahead, reasserting itself again and again throughout the national experience. This deep belief in freedom of opportunity perhaps explains the apparent inconsistency of the middle American in deploring job and housing discrimination while voicing considerable intolerance. He believes, as the Kerner commission reported, that ghetto conditions result as much from a lack of ambition and industriousness among their black residents as they do from white intolerance. There is confusion in the statistics as to the weight middle America accords environment and heredity, but there is no doubt of its strong conviction that the old tenement trail can work for any ethnic group.

Third, not only does a review of the polls suggest that the present majority views are more complicated than surface accounts make them but also when one dips back into older surveys, it is clear that these views are subject to substantial positive change.

In the fall of 1967, the *Public Opinion Quarterly*, making the first summary of race relations in five years, used housing—next to intermarriage, perhaps the most sensitive racial issue—as its point of reference. Gaffin, Gallup, Harris, NORC, Roper, and SRC polls were all recorded. From a battery of comparable NORC inquiries, the fraction of whites approving residential integration ran:

	Whites Nationwide	*Southern Whites*
1942	35%	12%
1956	51%	38%
1963	64%	51%

In 1944 (NORC), 69% of whites polled said it would make a strongly unfavorable difference to them if a Negro family moved next door; by 1958 (Gallup), this had dropped to 48%; by 1963 to 20%; and by 1967 to 12%.

John M. Orbell and Kenneth Sherrill have written a provocative analysis of racial attitudes of urban upper-middle and lower-middle class whites as they are related to the structure—that is, the homogeneity or diversity—of their own neighborhoods. Evaluating data from what must certainly be a middle America archetype—Columbus, Ohio—they found that resistance to residential integration *increased* as one got higher in the social economic scale and as the neighborhood became more homogeneous. Whites living in areas virtually without Negroes are more hostile when the areas are higher in class; but all are more hostile than whites in integrated neighborhoods.[20] Middle America in the combat zone of the changing neighborhood may feel insecure and sound racist, but those most ready to exclude blacks are the high-income residents of all-white areas. (Yes, Virginia, there is a lily-white suburb!)

So the neighborhood context, the life-style, the capability of leadership mold views as well as rigid class identification. These views change over time and seemingly become more tolerant. A core set of values continues that rejects the doctrine of a lumpenproletariat, black or white.

If we can take these as hopeful indications that a link with the majority in urban policy is possible, it becomes important to identify what it is that so infuriates the majority today.

The Issue of Procedure

Working through the attitude surveys of the last decade suggests that the old distinction between goals and means may be the critical factor. How Americans feel about equal rights, help to the poor, and nondiscrimination is one side of the ledger. How they feel about sit-ins, boycotts, protests, the whole "politics of disruption" is the other.

Again, Gallup, Harris, NORC, and SRC offer evidence. Polling throughout the period of civil right action in the early fifties shows a strong majority of whites *disapproving* of sit-ins, boycotts, picketing, and freedom rides. Seventy per cent disapproved of the famous and peaceful March on Washington in 1963.

On the whole, the more abrasive the tactics, the more negative the response. The boycott of manufacturers who do not hire enough black workers was opposed by 55% of whites polled, while 91% opposed lying down in front of trucks at construction sites to protest hiring discrimination.

Only when violent police action was directed at peaceful civil rights demonstrations—as in the televised disgraces in Birmingham and at the Selma bridge—has the average American sided with the demonstrators. A poll just after the showdown in Selma showed 48% of

the country siding with the demonstrators and only
21% with the state of Alabama.[21]

In a Harris poll in December, 1966, white reaction
was sought to a long list of black leaders actively identified with the effort to secure equal rights. With two
impeccably moderate exceptions, Thurgood Marshall
and Roy Wilkins, each of these men was thought by a
strong majority of those responding to have "hurt the
Negro cause more than he helped."

Most of the silent majority, the polls suggest, ac-
knowledge the inequities between black and white in
jobs, housing, and education. They believe in the capacity of government to change things in these areas.
But they also believe in established procedures, cus-
tomary ways of doing things, orderly routes to redress,
such as legal suits and standing for election. Aggres-
sive, unconventional, disruptive tactics are counter-
productive to the majority's disposition to change.

Perhaps Martin Lipset best summarizes the state
of mind of middle America when he contrasts the
mood of the country on issues and its mood regarding
the process of their resolution. Antiwar sentiment, he
points out, is sharply on the rise, but the increase in
distaste for antiwar demonstrations is even sharper. A
continuing although slightly declining commitment to
integration accompanies a sharply rising hostility to
riots. The majority of Americans, Lipset believes, are
left on the issues and *right* on the tactics. So by virtue
of its behavior the militant left puts the right in power

when, in terms of programs, the right does not command the majority.[22] Ideological liberals, in Lipset's view, drive out their practical brothers.

Innovative politics need not forever be limited to minority, elite, professional politics. The record suggests that they can command the support of the majority. But they have to work. In the real world of expanding population, deteriorating housing, group anxieties, individual frustrations and tensions, mediocre public services, insufficient foresight, and inadequate funds, whatever the majority supports must in a relatively short time be proven feasible. This is, of course, the great danger of environmental politics as Swift points out.[23]

Politicians will have to face up to some extremely awkward decisions, for instance, whether to ban cars without anti-pollution devices. There will have to be international agreements in which short-term national interests have to be sacrificed. It means, in short, a more responsible view of man's relationship to his habitat.

If a more responsible view is to be taken of the American environment, it might as well include the American city. Not the *will*, as so many have claimed, is lacking; not the inherent tolerance, decency, reasonableness, or flexibility of most of the American people. The *way* is what is difficult, and we must ask ourselves if the trained, educated, skilled programmers of urban redevelopment are equal to the task.

Chapter VIII

A Relevant Definition
of the City

We have then considered and rejected two explanations of our present urban situation:

—*The Mistaken Observations Theory.* This theory
says that our urban difficulties arise chiefly from a
lower class, incapable of improvement, implacably
expanding and more dangerous at close quarters in
the city than it was on the farm.

—*The Unworkable System Theory.* This theory suggests that "majoritarian democracy" must be replaced by "pluralistic democracy"—i.e., grouping
minorities by function and area in such ways as to
provide them distinctive command of their interests. Otherwise, inner city ghetto minorities will always be outvoted.

In their places, we have examined two admittedly
partial explanations from a partial political science:

—*The mismatch between the character of the problems involved and the nature of responses devised.* Policymakers have too often prescribed economic medicine for political needs, and vice-versa. The relative weighting of resource allocation and institutional changes was often faulty.

—*The complications inherent in a majoritarian system working on a minority problem.* The critical factor is how minority needs are presented to a majority and coupled with them, not the impossibility of gaining majority approval. This requires skill and leadership of special proportions.

Now we arrive at the hard stage of prescription, an operating program, the way that can mobilize the national majority will. The "policy process" in national domestic affairs that sends an idea rollicking along by trade-offs and compromises from formal legislative introduction through committees and floor debate to enactment and a victorious bill-signing ceremony, Rose-Garden-White House style, is real enough as an exercise of political power and influence. But it is unreal in the sense that at that point nothing has happened: The idea is still a piece of paper. In modeling terms, one man's system is another man's environment, and we are concerned here with both—cities and city politics.

In going then from an enacted idea to a tangible change in the physical or social environment, more is

involved than turning the matter over to the professional administrator, depositing it in the bureaucracy,
or hiring an outside organization and expecting results.
Old bureaucracies are masters at making new programs identical to old ones and playing *their* games of
internal politics. So are private entrepreneurs accept-
ing public business. It is at the point of impact with the
"real" system that the pains and pleasures of the political system are felt and recorded. It is when a policy is
translated into a project—tangible, visible, existent—
that problems are actually being solved. But, first,
what *are* the urban "problems" that we are talking
about? This needs to be precisely understood.

The City as Stage

Perhaps the most troublesome analytical problem
in facing up to the urban condition has been the failure
to define the city clearly, and, hence, clarify the nature
of city problems and the "crisis."

For the most part, observers saw the growing
urban populations and expanding urban areas as creat-
ing or embodying a series of problems: deteriorating
housing, poor city services, fragmented local governments, sprawl, congestion, poverty, underemployment.
After Detroit and Newark, journalists quickly turned
these problems into "crises": the traffic crisis, the wel-

fare crisis, the crime crisis, the population crisis, the black-white crisis, the housing crisis, the why-can't-Johnny-read crisis. To all intents and purposes, the city became a stage across which marched all the great national issues of the day. Add the adjective "urban" to a problem and you had a crisis. Dump the crises helter-skelter in a single drawer labeled "city" and the field of urban affairs was established.

Now the city treated as a stage for America's woes has dramatic unity and appeal. Intellectually, however, the concept is an analytic and programmatic nightmare. It is as if the nation would not have to wrestle with the question of industrial organization and control if all factories were in the hinterland; would not have to debate our defense posture if all ABM sites were restricted to the Dakotas; and would not have to come to grips with educational requirements in a technological society if all our public schools were rural.

Treated as a stage, urbanism is all-embracing, incapable of intellectual appreciation. That concept plays hob as well with efforts to attack specific urban ills. The failure in the poverty program to recognize that the needs of the urban poor are not the same as urban needs, the inability to handle highways designed for the wide open spaces in urban neighborhoods, the effort to design educational aid programs that would simultaneously help the farm child in Mississippi and the city child in Camden—all flow from this first careless and then popularized misconception. Tying up all our ills in one bag and calling it urban does not advance the state of urban scholarship.

Another formulation of "the city"—less romantic and perhaps more helpful, certainly more abstract, more theoretical—was first expressed in *Science and the City*, the report of the 1966 conference of urbanists, scientists, and engineers cosponsored by the Office of Science and Technology and HUD. That conference chose to treat the city as a place where people lived in such density, with such a high level of human interactions that their behavior is changed and the ordinary biological and physical properties of the space they inhabit are changed as well. Subsequent inquiries would amend that formulation: Interactions of urban people are especially dependent on high technology communications these days, the information imparted increasingly involves consumption instead of production, and the capacity for immobilizing or disrupting these interactions is very great. Finally, second- and third-order consequences make it imperative to consider urban development in systematic terms. The basic formulation remains the same, however: Different levels of density make for different behavior as well as differences in the physical and biological environments. So, for example, automobile exhausts that are harmless on a country road are, of course, dangerous pollutants on the urban expressways. Dogs can roam at will on the prairie; they are leashed on Park Avenue. Village idiots can manage life in a New England town; they cannot manage on the sidewalks of Chicago. Deviant social behavior unnoticed in the cornfields invades the values of others where others are around.

In short, life speeds up in the urban world; attitudes, actions, decisions ricochet off other human beings. There are different requirements for conduct vocationally and socially, different uses of fauna and foliage, different management of physical space. Most of all, the importance of elemental competence is magnified; John Gardner's quest for excellence comes close to being an imperative.

Now strangely perhaps, the rejection of the city-as-stage perspective, and the recourse to the more abstract density-space formulation impels our attention to the human side of city building. It concentrates analysis on the person and his relation with others. Even as contemporary protestors decry the antiseptic dispassionate cast of social science, their humanistic impulses detract us from man and direct us toward nature in the physical sense. Meantime, the social scientist continues to contend that the measure is man.

More exactly, what the density-space approach yields is a departure point for public policymaking and intervention that is both people-oriented and empirically susceptible to verification, both relevant and feasible.

In this context, urban policy begins with the number and movement of peoples; population patterns and

migration patterns. Who moves and why and where?
What frictions accompany human interactions today?
What barriers and constraints intrude on free movement? What is the optimum level of density? How
many Americans can the country support?

Now it is true that these issues of population
growth and movement are also susceptible to sensa-
tionalism. Ben Wattenberg capsuled the problem of demographic emotionalism in what he termed "the nonsense explosion," where he protested the vision of
crowded, crowded, crowded America. He writes: [24]

> While rhetoric rattles on about where will we ever put the
> next hundred million Americans, while the President tells
> us that the roots of so many of our current problems are to
> be found in the speed with which the last hundred Ameri-
> cans came upon us, while the more apocalyptic demogra-
> phers and biologists . . . are talking about putting nonexis-
> tent birth control chemicals in the water supply and about
> federal licensing of babies—the critical facts in the argu-
> ment remain generally unstated. . . .
>
> The critical facts are that America is not by any stan-
> dard a crowded country and that the American birth rate
> has been at an all time low. . . .

Wattenberg's defusing of the population time-
bomb is helpful as is redefining the environmental crisis to include people and housing. Nevertheless, after
all probable discounts for declining fertility rates, later
marriages, and revived faith in the pill are made, the
United States will still have to settle sizable millions of

people in urban circumstances in the next generation. The year 2000 may see only 285 million Americans instead of 308 million, but even the lowest census projections add the entire current population of Great Britain to our present headcount in three decades. By 1980, the best estimate is for 30 million additional Americans and 43 million additional *urban* Americans as the cities continue to work as suction pumps drawing in poor farmers.

Moreover, 1968 Department of Agriculture figures confirm the trends Martin Meyerson first characterized as the "Rim Theory" of urban migration. Comparing the 1950 and 1960 censuses, Meyerson suggested that the great midwestern heartland was emptying out, absolutely in terms of rural population, and relatively in terms of urban population, and that the coastal metropolitan areas were capturing the lion's share of growth and redistribution, thereby enlarging Gottman's megalopoli by a rate of 3 to 1 compared to the national average growth. Jerome Pickard refined and extended Meyerson's initial thesis and in the mid-sixties projected some twelve major megalopoli where jobs and homes would seem to concentrate. The recent agriculture projections make some further modifications: The rise of Atlanta, for example, has served as a stabilizer to eastern coastal flows, and the development of Arizona has had a similar western impact.

But by and large, the continued economic dominance of the urban Goliaths and the stability and de-

cline of America's old breadbasket seem established, if
the natural juices of the market place are allowed to
flow.

If these juices are allowed to flow, one can project
that:

—More and more of the next 85 to 100 million urban
Americans will live in outer reaches of existing
metropolitan areas in lower densities than present
ones but larger aggregates. The Californiazation
that Gottman now believes to threaten Europe
will be ubiquitous on this continent.

—The relative productive advantages in the private
sector of the larger cities that Raymond Vernon
and Edgar Hoover first explained for the New York
region and upon which Wilbur Thompson has bril-
liantly elaborated, will be maintained or increased.

—The social and political "discontinuities"—i.e., tensions, confrontations, conflicts, discomforts, anxieties—will rise.

—The special issues of the identity of person and the
advancement of the minority will remain to be
coped with, either by personal or neighborhood
adaptation.

—The maximization of economic values will preclude
achievement of other values; disproportional increase in local and state taxes will go on but so will
majority indignities and minority deprivations.

From Analysis to Intervention

Suppose we seek to alter these migration patterns and reduce the frictions and discontent by common action? On the basis of our experience in the sixties, suppose we undertake to devise public policies that engage the support of the majorities and are innovative in the sense that they are funded from economic surpluses and do not challenge too many interests too directly. At the same time, suppose we try to seek security and attention to process for the majority and rapid visible progress economically and educationally, as well as political impact for the minority.

The Kennedy-Johnson legacy gives us a potpourri of program prototypes from which to choose:

—Physical development via housing subsidies, renewal, and metropolitan planning.

—Social development via citizen action and educational reform.

—Economic development via retraining, community enterprises, welfare reform, income reallocation, and labor innovation.

—Intelligent coordination of the sort that model cities and councils of government were originally supposed to produce.

And there are more radical proposals: banning automobiles downtown, revenue-sharing, guaranteed annual wage. Combined imaginatively, administered and funded well, these constitute a large and varied enough assortment to be politically viable to our majoritarian-distributive requirement. The difficulty is that they do not address the problem of population growth and movement. They take the present needs of present communities as given. They try to improve existing circumstances but they would not alter them. They do not constitute an urban strategy.

Chapter IX

A Strategy Based on Land

Now a workable public strategy in its most elemental form is a judicious mix of resource allocations and regulatory authority. Government increases inducements by tax or payment for certain kinds of voluntary private decisions, and it forecloses or constrains certain other decisions. Both actions are taken in the name of the public interest.

In the past, it is commonplace that we have subsidized housing and urban highway development, regulated transportation by public utility decree, traffic ordinances, and parking tickets, and maintained residential neighborhoods by housing and health codes. That is, government has left the economic development process to private decision-making but followed up those decisions by insuring shelter and public facilities—at least for middle America. In our present circumstances where it is population and job flows that are the key forces to influence, different uses of these basic techniques are appropriate. Subsidies in the development of new communities should be provided, sufficient to offset the economic advantages to private entrepreneurs in existing metropolitan areas, on the grounds of eliminating some painful urban public external diseconomies. Increased regulatory activity is required in established metropolitan areas to improve existing conditions, especially with respect to the use of urban land.

This combination of subsidy and regulation in sufficient volume and intensity, together with institutional reform that responds to identity and political needs, could alter current demographic projections and change the quality of urban life.

Influencing Industrial Location

If we were colonists again, early in the process of industrialization, regulation of industry location—i.e., comprehensive national planning—might be a most appropriate policy technique. Indeed, for many developing countries today that would be a wise policy, coupled with heavy subsidies to urban services in existing cities to speed their transformation from market-barter economies to industrialized ones. One of the great limitations of our foreign aid policies over the past generation was that they were so focused on increasing agriculture productivity and controlling populations that we lost the opportunity to guide industrial location to new urban sites before urban economies were established in old ones.

That kind of opportunity does not exist in the United States today. The well-developed, expanding economic bases of existing cities, dependent on intricate, subtle, but vital relationships among firms and industries, labor markets and municipal services, produce, as Vernon and Hoover first demonstrated, important external economies to the firms there located. Although more and more industries are footloose (that is, increasingly indifferent to classic factors of raw materials, labor, and natural transportation advantages), a location in large metropolitan areas produces calculable advantages in cost reduction and product improvement and encourages managerial and labor recruitment. The existing stock of "natural monopolies"—libraries, schools, parks, universities—adds further benefits.

The incredible rebuilding of Manhattan from Forty-second Street to Fifty-ninth Street, which represented 60% of the new office construction in the *nation* in the 1950's, and the industrial boom of Boston's golden semicircle, Route 128, were not the result of capricious decisions. The economic advantages of large metropolitan areas to the private firm are demonstrable.

What are not yet demonstrable are the public *dis*economies. The high rents for offices in the Pan-American Building make clear the profitability of that private investment. What is not clear is the additional cost to the city in extra service requirements for water, safety, and transportation. Much less have we considered the ultimate public result of these privately rewarding decisions: A daytime population density such that, in event of an emergency evacuation, the surrounding streets would be three-deep in alarmed, frightened human beings.

Until the social indices that Raymond Bauer and others are working so intently to develop are operative, we cannot calculate these public diseconomies with precision. There are some good estimates derived from the municipal cost and expenditure literature in planning, but the relationships are not clear.

What we could do, however, in a rich economy, is assume the marginal value of these public diseconomies to equal the marginal value of the private economies and to subsidize in that amount, plus a factor, to build the economic basis of new communities, labor surplus neighborhoods in central cities, or designated rural growth centers.

Subsidies for New Communities

So far that sort of calculation has not entered directly into new communities planning. The 1966 and 1968 housing acts focused on the problems of the developer, in particular his cash flow situation over the extended period of early development. The liberalized mortgage guarantees of the 1966 act proved not to be a sufficient inducement. The 1968 act with its government debentures, deferred repayment, and correlated grants-in-aid for public facilities should be effective.

But the present law's impact could be expanded and accelerated if the developer could offer appropriate prospective industries subsidies that produced cost and transportation situations equal to those in suburban industrial parks today.

This summary proposition for new community industrial subsidies conceals a host of secondary issues and complexities. How is an eligible new community to be distinguished from a natural suburb? Are there requirements of relative isolation to be met, bonus points for manufacturing pioneers venturing into South Dakota and Wyoming? Should the subsidies be direct or through that wondrous instrument of the Internal Revenue Act, adjusting depreciation or capital credits? How much of the increased population should be accommodated in established communities? A new field day for lawyers, accountants, planners, and promoters is an inevitable consequence of this kind of a proposal.

Nonetheless, entrepreneurial activity is at the heart of the policy. The government compensates somewhat for risks; tilts the board in favor of new patterns of plant location; perhaps slows the rate of industrial expansion for a time, at least as measured by conventional indices of the Council of Economic Advisers. But over the long term, new, productive community development goes on, not harassed by insufficiencies of public investments.

The powerful inducement to take advantage of the economies that mature large regions offer is offset. And those old regions get a chance to catch their breath; a pause in the relentless push of growth and migration may allow them to plan, think, and program in place of ceaseless improvisation.

Government interventions of this nature do not have to be confined to new communities or started from scratch. Old, middle-sized cities, once flourishing, now economically depressed, could be recipients of subsidies on the grounds that their social diseconomies are not large—or indeed approach equilibrium with private economies. With this kind of support Savannah, Utica, Scranton, Fall River all could rise again. Replacing the less attractive inducements of cheap labor and local tax rebates that bring marginal industries into small towns or declining regions would be incentives for first-rate industries to help build first-rate towns.

Regulations for Old Communities

Along with carrots to direct population and job flows out of their present channels by location subventions come sticks to improve life in the marvelously proficient but too often uncomfortable and dangerous established urban regions. One can conceive of all kinds of regulations that might command the support of majority and minority and better the lives of all. They would range from measures to increase the liquidity of home equities to equalization of school expenditures in metropolitan areas to more police on the streets to more stringent planning requirements that force incoming industries to pay for some of the additional costs they generate that are not calculated in property assessments.

But the regulatory measure most urgently required is the control of spiraling urban land prices. In 1969, the Kaiser committee reported land to be the fastest rising element of all major housing costs, with the average site value of a new FHA-insured house up from $1,035 in 1950 to $3,766 in 1967, or from 12% to 20% of total cost. The Douglas commission found that the value of ordinary taxable real estate rose from $269 billion in 1956 to $523 billion in 1966, an average of $25 billion a year or a per family increase of $5,000. While the wholesale price index rose annually at 1%, and the consumer index 1.8%, the increase in land value in that period was 6.9%.

At the cutting-edge of suburbia, where rural land was transformed into urban land, the estimated rise in value was 130%, an average per land parcel of 6.2%. The classic study of Philadelphia land values by Grace Milgrams showed a 1,460% rise in twenty years of suburban development.

These spiraling costs affect both majority and minority. By 1969, despite an automatic write-down in renewal land value to $500 per unit where central-city
residential reuse was involved, New York, Philadelphia, Boston, and San Francisco were finding it impossible to come in under total unit cost limits for low-income housing. The dilemma of the national policymaker was that with a fixed dollar appropriation for
renewal, further write-downs by federal subsidy (in
some cases the local request was for complete or negative write-offs) reduced the total number of units to be
built nationwide. The agony of the locality was the political impossibility of a big-city mayor saying he could
build no more housing for the poor.

And out in the suburbs, rising land values made
the cost of building sites the biggest cost booster in
housing: from 15% to 32% of a finished family dwell-
ing. With the average home cost rising from $11,300 in
1952 to $17,000 in 1965, and to $23,000 in 1969, only
changes in down payment requirements, extension in
mortgage life, and other financial and administrative
changes kept monthly payment levels manageable.

The changes in land values raise in sharp relief the
old issue of the speculators' role, in contrast to that of
the entrepreneur.

Senator Douglas and a minority of his commission
waxed indignant on this point.[25]

The owners of the land can go to Hawaii, rest languidly on
the beaches or make prolonged safaris into the inmost re-

gions of Africa. They may study Shakespearian literature at Stratford-on-Avon, or Zen Buddhism in Japan, or ponder urban problems in Washington. . . . they will become richer and richer without toil or sweat.

That view is not universally shared. As Sylvan Kamm of the Urban Institute has pointed out: [26]

As a class, investors in underdeveloped land do not make enormous gains and may indeed lose money. There are many risks . . . and among the most important are the thinness of the market . . . illiquidity and the general lack of market information.

These conditions lead to a heavy discount rate, with a large component due to uncertainty and illiquidity, and these departures from fluctuable markets —not capitalist exploitation—are the prime sources of urban land inflation.

One can also count on the interplay of politics and economics in shoving up land prices. It is public investments—highways, water and sewer lines, industrial parks—that create value. Anticipating growth is increasingly a local political strategy, rewarding to officeholder and landowner alike.

Whatever the sources, however, it seems clear that the rapid climb in land values already precludes a wide range of housing choices in older parts of a metropolitan area; it complicates the process of natural or programmed renewal; it encourages further suburban spread; and it adds accordingly to public infrastructure costs. While the impact is not so great on commercial and industrial location, it is heavy on residential and public construction. *Regulatory intervention that controls land values is probably the most important single factor in altering the marginal development of settled urban regions.*

Now a first reaction to this strategy can understandably be a yawn: The call for reform in land management and taxation is not new.

Henry George revisited; Kenneth Galbraith's search for public monies from an overstuffed private sector; the Pittsburgh differential land tax plan; transaction taxes on land value increases to tap parts of the increase value of the $70 billion worth of real estate that changes hands annually (somewhere between $15 and $20 billion); special assessments for socially induced land values—these have been a regular part of the urban reformers' agenda. In recent years, the agenda has also included advance public purchases of land, public ownership with leaseback arrangements to private parties, and freezes on land values when public purposes are declared.

It is not the technical merits or demerits of the various proposals, certainly not the call again for a single tax (our needs have gone beyond that sensible proposal of a simpler day), that is our central concern. *It is the need for a land reform program in urban America.*

For a quarter of a century, the United States has agitated for land reform around the world. We imposed land reform on defeated Japan; tried to break up estates in South America and South Asia; advanced new schemes in Africa; applauded public regulatory practices in Europe that accelerated postwar city rebuilding in the Marshall Plan era; and approved Scandinavian land developments that rested on socialistic doctrines of public land ownership. But we never practiced what we preached, and we now see the consequences in our urban backyards.

Tax policies that recapture increased land values derived from public investments are a minimum requirement, together with differential assessments of improvements and sites. The establishment of land exchange banks to reduce suburban discount rates seems likewise obvious. These are passive, however, in terms of minority needs for low-income housing and general metropolitan planning.

The financial impact of changes in land taxing policy alone is impressive. An economist in Milwaukee studied the effect of removing property taxes on improvements and taxing only according to the community-created location value of the site. His conclusion was that such a shift would mean that it would pay owners of obsolete downtown buildings to tear them down and replace them with new buildings that made better use of the site. This without subsidy of any kind.[27] More intensive redevelopment downtown would serve to reduce both commercial sprawl and suburban land prices.

Fundamentally, we are at the point where public

ownership and public planning are probably the essential components for a genuine land reform program. Certain levels of density no longer make tolerable private ownership and development even though zoning and planning requirements are available to affect them indirectly. Only a general plan with land ownership and control being the decisive forces in critical areas can do the job. Otherwise Charles Abrams' depiction of squatters around the world will become a part of the American scene as well. Indeed, this is probably a prime factor in the trailer home explosion of the last five years. The principal difference is that our squatters are motorized.

Some Indispensable Conditions

To conclude a long and complex recitation of the present conditions of America's greatest problem—life in its cities—with only two recommendations, industrial subsidies outside established urban areas and land reform within, may seem anticlimactic. Yet, detailed proposals along these lines would deeply shake the status quo and provoke considerable urban political debate.

I do not suggest that such measures displace the beginnings that were made in the sixties. The efforts at institutional change, decentralization to the ghetto neighborhood and the development of a two-tier metropolitan political system, should go forward. These efforts, over time, will restore the political muscle that atrophied when the municipal reformers did in the boss and will help readjust the balance with bureaucracies that are no longer so penetrable by patronage as they are made independent of public direction by being unionized. Economic development and renewal activities ought to go on as well. But the policies that matter most are going to be the policies that can *change* population patterns, not simply respond to them.

Finally, if no foray such as this aims at comprehensive treatment, neither can it pretend to specify its utopia. Henry Adams (angrily) struggled with our dynamo and turned largely back to the cathedral city of medieval Europe. I intend no such specifications as to the form and plan and style of the ideal American city. I would, however, suggest certain conditions as indispensable.

The first condition is that we husband and increase our resource of urban professionalism. The effort to rebuild old cities and make new ones has been and remains dependent on a thin red line of seasoned mayors, committed councilmen, energetic municipal department heads, effective planners, and imaginative developers. All are in short supply. While we enlarge the role of the citizen and make his/her voice more powerful in urban decision-making, we must recognize that the modern city cannot be run by volunteers. The

upgrading and expansion of professional urban man-
power must be given a high national priority.

The second condition is that the ideology of distributive politics be subdued to the point that innovative politics are possible. If we fall victim to the belief
that the only thing government does well is raise taxes
and redistribute them, we are indeed at the mercy of
the market place.

The final condition is that the majority as well as
the minority be engaged. Response to the minority will
not be enough. The fringe benefits that flow to the
working American, the suburbanite, the second- and
the third-generation ethnic, must be visible and demonstrable.

If there is no blueprint for the American city, if
we can describe only the haziest parameters, perhaps
there is comfort in the fact that even our medieval
brethren saw the city more in terms of content than of
form.

In the fourteenth century, William Langland
wrote of his aspiration for man in a collective social
state. He began with these words:

> I looked eastward toward the sun
>   and saw a tower. As I saw it, Truth
>   dwelleth within it.

> I looked toward the west in a little while
>   and saw a deep dale.
> Death and wicked spirits lived in those dwellings.

A Fair Field of Folk Found I Between the Two

All manner of men
The mean and the rich
Working and wandering as the world asks.

A fair field of folk can be a city.

Notes

1. Ben H. Bagdikian, *The Information Machines* (New York, Harper and Row, 1971), p. 95.

2. E. B. White, *Here is New York* (New York, Harper, 1949), pp. 13–15.

3. Fred Powledge, "Going Home to Raleigh," *Harper's Magazine,* (April, 1970), Vol. 240, 55.

4. *Building the American City:* Report of the National Commission on Urban Problems to the Congress and to the President of the United States (Washington, D. C., U.S. Government Printing Office, 1968), p. 26.

5. Edward C. Banfield, *The Unheavenly City* (Boston, Little, Brown and Company, 1970), pp. 20–21.

6. *Ibid.,* p. 210.

7. *Ibid.,* p. 53.

8. John W. Gardner, *Excellence* (New York, Harper and Row, 1961).

9. Arthur R. Jensen, "How Much Can We Boost I.Q. and Scholastic Achievement?," *Harvard Educational Review,* XXXIX (Winter, 1969), 1–123.

10. David C. McClelland, *The Achieving Society* (New York, Nostrand, 1961); also (with D. G. Winter) *Motivating Economic Achievement* (New York, The Free Press, 1969).

11. *Report of the National Advisory Commission on Civil Disorders* (New York, Bantam Books, Inc., 1968), p. 483.

12. Herbert J. Gans, "We Won't End the Urban Crisis until We End 'Majority Rule,'" *New York Times Magazine* (August 3, 1969).

13. The members of the 1965 Task Force were Kermit Gordon, Charles Haar, Ben Heineman, Edgar Kaiser, William Rafsky, Walter Reuther, Senator Abraham Ribicoff, and Whitney Young. The 1964 Task Force included Katherine Bauer, Jerome Cavanaugh, Nathan Glazer, Joseph Kennedy, Saul Klaman, Ralph McGill, Karl Menninger, Martin Myerson, Raymond Vernon, and Paul Ylvisaker.

14. *The London Observer*, (February 1, 1970).

15. "The Troubled American," *Newsweek*, LXXIV (October 6, 1969), 32–33.

16. Gans, "Urban Crisis," *New York Times Magazine*, p. 12, 14.

17. "The Troubled American," *Newsweek*, pp. 35, 45.

18. *Ibid.*, p. 46.

19. Angus Campbell and Howard Schulman, *Racial Attitudes in 15 American Cities* (Ann Arbor, Michigan, Survey Research Center, 1968).

20. John M. Orbell and Kenneth Sherrill, "Racial Attitudes in the Metropolitan Context: a Structural Analysis," *Public Opinion Quarterly*, XXXIII (Spring, 1969), 46–52.

21. Hazel Erskine, "The Polls: Demonstrations and Race Riots," *Public Opinion Quarterly*, XXXI (Spring, 1968).

22. This is based on personal conversation with Professor Lipset, but similar ideas are developed in Seymour Martin Lipset and Gerald Schaflander, *Passion and Politics: Student Activism in America,* (Boston, Little, Brown and Company, 1971), Chapter VII.

23. *The London Observer,* (February 1, 1970).

24. Ben Wattenberg, "The Nonsense Explosion," *New Republic,* CLXII (April 4 and 11, 1970), 18–23.

25. *Building the American City,* p. 396.

26. Sylvan Kamm, "Reducing Land Costs through Improvements in the Market Mechanism: a Potential System of Land Exchange Banks," Working Paper 112-10 (Washington, D. C., The Urban Institute, 1970).

27. Mason Gaffney, "The Adequacy of Land as a Tax Base," in David Holland, ed., *The Assessment of Land Value* (Madison, University of Wisconsin Press, 1970), pp. 179, 192–95. See also Gaffney, "Land Planning and the Property Tax," *Journal of the American Institute of Planners,* XXXV, No. 3, 178–83.